# Discover how Jewish wisdom can shape your spiritual identity in an ever-changing world.

In ten brief chapters, each illuminating a core concept of Jewish spirituality, Arthur Green lays out his reasons for ongoing commitment to Jewish memory and Judaism's unique approach to universal truth. Drawing mainly from the Jewish mystical tradition, he presents in brief form gems of personal wisdom derived from ancient Kabbalistic writings and the Hasidic masters, even as he "opens the windows" to the spirit of change and new ideas from both East and West.

"Readable in a few hours but very possibly not forgotten thereafter…. A wealth of wisdom."

—**American Library Association's** *Booklist*

"Profound wisdom in a simple format…. Offer[s] readers easy access to Judaism's most novel ideas."

—**Dr. Kerry M. Olitzky**, executive director,
Big Tent Judasim; author, *Introducing My Faith and My Community:
The Jewish Outreach Institute Guide for the Christian in a Jewish
Interfaith Relationship*

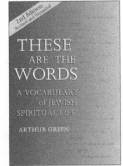

## Also Available by Arthur Green

**These Are the Words, 2nd Edition**
*A Vocabulary of Jewish Spiritual Life*

The basic vocabulary of Jewish spiritual life, explained with humor, insight and relevance.

6 x 9, 320 pp, Quality PB Original, 978-1-58023-494-8

# JUDAISM'S

# BEST
# IDEAS

*A Brief Guide for Seekers*

ARTHUR GREEN

For People of All Faiths, All Backgrounds
JEWISH LIGHTS Publishing

*Judaism's Ten Best Ideas:*
*A Brief Guide for Seekers*

2016 Quality Paperback Edition

**Library of Congress Cataloging-in-Publication Data**
Green, Arthur, 1941– author.
 Judaism's ten best ideas / Arthur Green.
    pages cm
  ISBN 978-1-58023-803-8 (quailty pbk)—
ISBN 978-1-58023-806-9 (ebook)  1. Judaism. 2. Jewish way of life.  I. Title.
  BM562.G74 2014
  296.3—dc23
                            2014016092


Manufactured in the United States of America

Cover Design: Jenny Buono
Text Design: Tim Holtz

*For People of All Faiths, All Backgrounds*
Jewish Lights Publishing
www.jewishlights.com


ISBN 978-1-68442-292-0 (hc)

# Contents

# Introduction

**W**elcome to my short course in Jewish wisdom, the ten best ideas in Judaism. Over the course of the few pages before you, I hope to share with you what I consider the core of Jewish teaching, the ideas that represent the Jewish people's greatest ongoing contribution to human civilization. Of course, one could write a whole book—and a much longer one—about each of these ideas, detailing their origins, their subtle implications, and their applications to contemporary living. I have tried to give you a little bit of each in very brief form in this little volume you have just opened. But there is infinitely more to be said.

Some of these teachings take on the rarified air of theology, written and refined by Jewish thinkers over many centuries. But their true birthplace lies in concrete daily life. I have tried here to return them to the context of universal human experience, hoping that you too will be able to touch them in your own unique way. They are often best expressed in stories, the most natural vehicle of teaching in our tradition. They may originate in a very defined and specific Jewish context, but I believe their wisdom radiates beyond all borders, and they are offered here for seekers everywhere.

I consider this to be a very personal little book. The Judaism presented in these pages is very much my own understanding of our tradition. It is what I have distilled from half a century of study and teaching, translating our sacred texts, and training rabbis. If someone at the end of this journey asks me, "Was it worth it?" this book is my answer. It is especially influenced by the mystical teachings of Hasidism, a movement of spiritual reawakening that began in eighteenth-century Eastern Europe. Hasidism is the version of Jewish teaching that has most powerfully spoken to my heart. But I have also tried to make this truly simple wisdom fully accessible to you, no matter who you are: Jew or non-Jew, old or young, scholar or seeker, committed practitioner looking for a fresh way to see what is already too familiar, or wanderer knocking on our tradition's door for the first time. Welcome to you all!

# SIMḤAH

## Joy

### Happiness as a Religious Precept

Imagine a religion that begins with "God wants you to be happy!" Beware of anything that threatens to take away your joy. In the end it will probably take you away from God as well. *Simḥah*, or joy, is the attitude toward life that Judaism seeks to instill. Despite the fact that Jewish history has more than its share of bleak and depressing chapters, the tradition sees itself as a joyous one. "Serve Y-H-W-H* with joy; come before God with singing." As the angels (literal or metaphorical, as you prefer)

---

\* Y-H-W-H is the mysterious, untranslatable divine name. We'll get to it in our final chapter. You may replace it with "God" or "the Lord," but I prefer not to. I promise to tell you why.

3

exult in the privilege of calling out "Holy, Holy, Holy" each day before the divine throne, we too are called upon to rejoice in the gift of knowing God, of loving God's creation, and of attesting to the divine presence that fills this world, both within us and around us.

This way of living is particularly emphasized in the Hasidic tradition, a form of Judaism that broke away from a growing tendency toward self-punishment that seems to be the shadow side of most religions.

Rabbi Israel Ba'al Shem Tov, the first great master of Hasidism, taught us to turn away from that shadow. Y-H-W-H created human beings, becoming present in the human soul, he taught, so that we might serve God in joy. The key biblical verse here reads "May the God-seekers' heart rejoice" (1 Chron. 16:10). Seeking God itself is an act that is to fill the heart with joy. *The delight is not only in the finding but also in the seeking*.

The great enemy of such a joyous quest is self-doubt, often caused by excessive worry about one's sins. Too much concern about sin puts you in mortal danger. The greatest trick of the evil forces, the Ba'al Shem Tov taught, is to make you worry about some small transgression you committed. That worry occupies your mind, takes you away from joy, and leaves you unable to see the beauty and wonder that always surround you. This leaves you feeling empty and hence unable to pray or to feel the warmth of God's presence. Your distance from God only grows greater, until you find yourself alone and abandoned, ripe to be picked off by the forces of further temptation. To avoid this pattern, he taught, repent of your sin quickly, decide you will not repeat it, and go back to serving with as much wholeness and joy as you can muster. Love, the wonders of nature, music, dance, and the close companionship of friends are all there to keep you on the path of joy. Storytelling, including lots of humor, is also part of the therapy. A famous later Jewish writer called Sholom Aleichem, who grew up in the Hasidic part of Eastern Europe, used to say, "Laughing is good for you; doctors prescribe laughter."

Joy is a gift that comes to people in different measures. Some folks seem to be blessed with a radiant personality that fills up with joy at the slightest stimulation. Even living with what appear to be the heaviest burdens does not dampen their spirit. For others, achieving joy represents a lifelong struggle against a natural tendency toward depression. Moments of true joy in such lives are rare and long treasured; we have to cultivate them, nourish them, and make them grow.

Those who struggle for joy have a special master within the Hasidic tradition. Rabbi Nahman of Bratslav was a great-grandson and expected heir of the Ba'al Shem Tov. He tried to live as his revered ancestor had taught, filling each moment with simple joy, but it failed to work for him. When he opened his eyes to discover God's presence filling the world, he instead felt God's absence and his own abandonment. Nahman's teachings on the struggle for joy are especially moving because they are so personal. He insisted that you must never let up in the search, that you have to turn your own shadows into light. Don't ignore your sadness, he taught, but chase it in order to transform it into happiness. He offered a parable that describes you, his reader, as a person in a roomful of dancers, but standing on the sidelines because your mood is too dark to let you enter the circle. Finally, someone grabs you by the hand (and this book may just be that "grab"), forcing you to join in the dance. As you warm up and begin to move, you notice your former sadness still standing back there on the side, looking somewhat disapprovingly at this new behavior and just waiting for you to stumble or feel self-conscious. The real task, says Rabbi Nahman, is to force that sadness itself into the circle and to make *it* dance, to see that it too is transformed into joy.[1]

*Simḥah shel mitzvah*, "joy of the commandment," is essential to the religious life as Judaism views it. A *mitzvah* may be a ritual form or an act of kindness to others. The point is that doing it is meant to fill our hearts with joy. A *mitzvah* is a place where you can meet God; *of course* it makes you happy. We anticipate it and look forward to fulfilling it. It's true that the sources also speak of the "yoke of the commandments," but the following story illustrates the sort of yoke they mean.

It is a pious custom to bake special matzahs right on the eve of Passover, in order to be engaged fully in the celebration of our freedom. To make matzah properly, you need to use water that has been left standing overnight, to ensure its absolute stillness. Once in the old country, where water was still brought from the river, an elderly rabbi was seen carrying two heavy buckets full of water for this purpose tied to a yoke around his neck. A neighbor riding by in a horse-drawn cart saw him and said, "Come here, rabbi! Put your buckets on my wagon, and we'll give you a ride." The rabbi looked up, smiling, and said: "I have the joy of doing this *mitzvah* only once a year, and you want me to give it away to a horse?"[2]

Here the burden itself has become a source of joy. When the ancient Israelites wandered through the wilderness for forty years, a certain group of Levites were given the privilege of carrying the Holy Ark. "How heavy it must have been," somebody commented, "with those

massive stone tablets inside it!" "No," a Levite answered.
"The Ark carried those who bore it."[3]

The same is true of any *mitzvah* carried out with joy.
It elevates and "carries" the one who does it.

"The world is like a wedding feast," the Talmud
teaches. Like good guests at the wedding, we are there
to rejoice over everything at once. We love the music,
the dancing, the special food and drink. We are happy
for the companionship of family and good friends. Still
more, we are happy for the bride and the groom and
anticipate the further happiness their life together will
bring to them and those around them. We rejoice at once
over all the goodness and blessing of life.[4] Among those
blessings is that of our own awareness of how blessed we
are and our ability to express our gratitude for life's many
gifts. That is the way we are supposed to feel about the
opportunity of doing a *mitzvah*.

A joyous occasion like a wedding, a birth, or another
happy event in the life of a family is referred to among
Jews simply as a *simḥah*, a joy. When we see one another
at sad moments, especially at a funeral or when visiting
a house of mourning, we express the wish to be with one
another in better times. *Nor oif simḥas* in Yiddish is the
way we say it: I hope to see you again, but "only at joys!"

# TZELEM ELOHIM

## Creation in God's Image

### What Are We Doing Here?

Two rabbis were having an argument some nineteen hundred years ago. The topic: What is Judaism's most important teaching? What is it all about? Rabbi Akiva, among the most famous of all our sages, had a ready answer: "'Love your neighbor as yourself' (Lev. 19:18) is the basic rule of Torah." His friend Simeon ben Azzai disagreed. "I know a more basic rule than that," he said. And he quoted: "This is the book of human generations: On the day God created humans, He created them in the image of God (*tzelem elohim*); male and female He created them, blessing them and calling them humans on the day they were created" (Gen. 5:1–2).[1]

What is the meaning of this debate, and what is its historical context? We should note first that Rabbi Akiva stands in a well-defined tradition. Almost two hundred years earlier, Hillel had said, when asked to summarize Judaism "while standing on one foot" for a potential convert: "Whatever is hateful to you, do not do to your neighbor. The rest is commentary; now go and study."[2] Akiva is simply turning Hillel's lesson around into the positive form. "Love is the most important teaching, and be sure to act on it. The rest will follow." Some readers may know of another Jewish teacher who lived at the midpoint between the two of them and said, "The first commandment is 'Hear O Israel, Y-H-W-H our God, Y-H-W-H is one. You shall love Y-H-W-H your God with all your heart, all your soul, and all your might.' The second is 'Love your neighbor as yourself.' There is no commandment greater than these."[3]

Akiva too seeks a Judaism based on love. Rabbi Akiva is in fact the great romantic figure of the rabbinic tradition. He is the one who insisted that while all of Scripture is holy, "the Song of Songs (the Bible's great poem about romantic love) is the Holy of Holies."[4] (The tale of Avika and his wife, Rachel, is perhaps the only true love story in the vast corpus of talmudic writings.) Even when Rabbi Akiva was being put to death by the Romans, he called out to his disciples: "Until now I never understood why Scripture tells us to love God with all your heart and all your soul. Is not the whole heart enough? But now I understand—even if He takes your soul, you love Him."[5] And with those words, he returned his soul to God.

Ben Azzai has two concerns with Akiva's formulation. The first is about love. How can I be *commanded* to love someone? There are, after all, some particularly unlovable human beings in this world. Certainly there are people who do some awfully unlovable things. Am I really transgressing all of Torah if I fail to love them? Suppose my neighbors act toward me in some vile and hateful way? Must I be expected to love them? Ben Azzai offers another answer: No, love is not required as the most basic rule of Torah. But remember that they are human beings, created in the image of God. Treat them that way, even if you can't love them. Human decency should not depend on our ability to muster a feeling of love for the other.

His second problem with Akiva's choice had to do with "neighbor." Suppose some follower of Akiva was to read that word to include only Jews? Or only pious, observant Jews? Or only people who interpreted the

Torah exactly as he did? Ben Azzai offers a principle to which there can be no exceptions, since it goes right back to Adam and Eve. *Every* human being is created in the image of God. Love them or not, neighbor or enemy, you must treat them all as you would treat God's image.

"Why are graven images forbidden by the Torah?" I once heard my great teacher Abraham Joshua Heschel ask. Why is the Torah so concerned with idolatry? You might think that it is because God has no image, and any depiction of God is therefore a distortion. But Heschel read the commandment differently. "No," he said, "it is precisely because God *has* an image that idols are forbidden. *You* are the image of God. Every human being is God's image. But the only way you can shape that image is by using the medium of your entire life. To take anything less than a full, living, breathing human being and try to create God's image out of it—that diminishes the divine and is considered idolatry." You can't *make* God's image; you can only *be* God's image.

What does the word *tzelem*, or "image," of God really mean? *Tzelem* is "image" in a representational sense, and it originally referred to the human form, both body and face. Hillel was once quoted as saying that a trip to the bathhouse was fulfilling a divine commandment, just like a loyal subject washing the statue of his king. Our body is part of God's image, and we need to maintain it with honor.[6] Some versions of the early Aramaic translation of the Torah occasionally translate *tzelem* with the Greek loan-word "icon"; every human being is God's icon. An icon, well known in the dominant culture in which Jews lived, is a depiction of God, a saint, or a holy scene that comes to bear within it the presence of that holy being, and hence is revered in itself. To call each person an icon of God is to say that each human both *resembles* and *contains* the divine form. Each person is to be held aloft, revered, and kissed, this ancient Jewish translation is suggesting, just as we have seen others do with *their* icons. (No wonder we have no images in the synagogue. The synagogue is filled with images of God as soon as we walk in!)

In later times, the notion of humans as the divine image was given a host of more abstract explanations. We are beings of intellect, conscience, moral freedom, responsibility, and lots more. But the idea that God somehow wanted this world to be populated with these godlike beings called humans always persisted. It can be seen in the blessings for fertility recited at a Jewish wedding and in the abhorrence the rabbinic tradition developed for killing, including the use of the death penalty. Our task is to see that there is *more* divine image in the world, not less.

The Torah commands that a criminal's body not be left hanging overnight, because "a hanging man is a curse of God" (Deut. 21:23). The sages interpret this to mean that God is somehow degraded when the human body, one that looks like God, is defiled. They daringly compare this to a tale of twin brothers, one of whom becomes king and the other a brigand. The brigand is properly caught and hanged for his crimes. But the king orders his body to be cut down, lest onlookers get the wrong idea.[7] A similar theme occurs in a tale of Adam's creation. The angels saw him, it is told, and sought to call out "Master!" thinking Adam was God. God had to diminish Adam, cut him down to size, so to speak, so there would be no mistake. The human being, *every* human being, somehow "looks" like God.[8]

There is an old Hasidic story about Reb Nahman Kossover, a friend of the Ba'al Shem Tov. Reb Nahman believed that the proper way to remain close to God was to constantly contemplate the four-letter name Y-H-W-H, to see the letters of God's name ever before him. He was a preacher, and when he looked out at his audience, he was able to see God's name in every face. But then times changed; the preacher was forced to become a merchant in order to survive. In the market-place, with the rapid pace of all the buying and selling, he found it harder to always concentrate on the name of God. So we are told that he hired a special assistant to follow him wherever he went. That person's only job was to be a reminder. Whenever he looked at his assistant's face, he would remember the name of God.[9]

What do you think that person (almost surely a man) looked like? Given the values of traditional Jewish society, he was probably not especially beautiful. Might he have been exceptionally tortured? Was it a tormented face that reminded the rabbi of God? Or was it something less dramatic, what in Yiddish might be called *eydelkeyt*, a combination of gentleness, warmth, and nobility? We'll never know, of course. Maybe it was just an ordinary human face, another person made in God's image. But he was there to serve as a reminder, and that was quite enough.

The faith that every human being is created in God's image is the part of Judaism that has taken the deepest root in what may be culturally characterized as the "Jewish soul." Ironically it continues to exist even in Jews who are not sure if they can still use the word *God* or *soul* in any other part of their vocabulary. But they still affirm the lesson of *tzelem elohim*, the truth that every human life is sacred. It calls us to boundless respect for each human life, a valuing of human difference and individuality, and a commitment to fair and decent treatment for each person.

This ancient Jewish belief has been reinforced by the equally ancient recall of Jewish suffering. The memory of slavery and liberation from Egypt, reinforced at every Passover table, is carved deeply into our souls, more deeply than we can see. It is no accident that bearers of Jewish names have been prominent in all modern movements for civil and human rights, including some that have turned sour. Many who carry those names are directly inspired by Jewish teaching; others, perhaps a majority, bear with them only a vague notion of Jewish tribal identity, especially the memory of persecution. Cognizant of their own ancestors' sufferings, they seek to avoid such a fate for others. The fact that a large majority of American Jews, despite their rising economic fortunes, continue to support liberal and generous programs of social welfare for the poor and needy also speaks to our ongoing proclamation of this truth.

Faith in *tzelem elohim* does not in itself resolve all our moral dilemmas. It can surely be argued that well-meaning people on both sides of such vexing contemporary issues as abortion, the right to die, the justification for war, and other difficult moral questions may bear the same legacy of faith in the sanctity of each human life.

But it does demand of us that whatever position we take on these and many other matters be rooted in the truth that our Torah, reinforced by Ben Azzai, declared our most basic principle so many generations ago.

# HALAKHAH
## Walking the Path
## A Community of Doers

*(handwritten margin notes: "Practice not theory?" and other annotations)*

Judaism sees itself as a path of praxis, and the Jews, or "Israel," as a human community that lives in accord with God's Torah as passed on, refined, and interpreted by an ongoing body of teachers and students. This body begins with what later memory called the Men of the Great Assembly, possibly reaching back to the time of Ezra and the beginning of the Second Temple, about 500 BCE. Later it was called the Sanhedrin, the great court of seventy-one rabbis that existed into the second century of the Common Era. After that it was the heads of the great academies; then just well-known rabbis scattered around the Jewish world who determined exactly how the life of Torah was to be practiced in ever-changing particular circumstances.

*Halakhah*, or the normative praxis of Judaism, is often rendered in English as "Jewish law." I, for one, regret that translation. The word *halakhah* literally means "walking," and it refers to a "path" or "a way of walking" in the world. It comes to us from the Torah when Moses, in the course of his final speeches, admonishes Israel "to walk in God's ways" (Deut. 10:12). In the original context, this probably means something very similar to "do what is good and upright" (Deut. 12:28), a moralistic admonition to good behavior. Much of this had to do with the imitation of God: Just as God is gracious and merciful, so you be gracious and merciful.[1] Or, even more specifically, referring to various biblical stories: Just as God feeds the hungry, clothes the naked, visits the sick, and buries the dead, so shall you do each of these as well.[2]

But people need more definition. Precisely *how* is one to walk in God's ways? Both in the ethical realm (those commandments that obligate us toward our fellow humans) and in the ritual realm (those acts that tie us to God) the Torah makes specific demands. Later traditions evolved that either expanded upon the biblical text or seemed to diverge from it. Questions were raised, discussed by scholars in great detail, and their answers were recorded, first by oral memory and later in writing. Then they were codified so that students and later generations could find and follow them with greater ease.

All this sounds an awful lot like a legal process. Indeed it is one. Why, then, do I object to translating *halakhah* as "law"? The word *law* has a cold and impersonal feel to it. You must do something because the law requires it. If not, your deviation from the norm makes you liable for punishment. Conforming to the law in our society requires no sense of commitment, no sense of personal engagement. It is simply what you do to avoid paying a fine or going to jail. Most people, if they can avoid getting caught, actually care little about conforming to the law.

*Halakhah,* especially in our modern world, is quite different. We choose to follow it out of personal commitment; it is our way of expressing such deep feelings as our love of God, our attachment to the legacy of the Jewish people, and our sense of the need to apply our spiritual beliefs to the conduct of even the most mundane human affairs. Despite the sometimes harsh biblical language, most of us know that *halakhah* has no punishing arm other than our own conscience. The decision to live within it, to whatever extent we do, is one that has to be made and renewed, sometimes questioned and revised, even on a daily basis. Our choice to stay on the path or to wander off it involves much more than the word *law* usually connotes.

The ancient rabbis debated the question of whether halakhic behavior required intentionality. Do the commandments require intent in order to be fulfilled?[3] Although the circumstances of each case vary, generally the rabbis came down on the side of not requiring intent. Who can know, after all, what goes on inside a person's heart? To put the matter in a contemporary and not specifically Jewish context, we might frame the question this way: Suppose you are in the Scouts and your troop is working in the city. You stop to help a blind person cross the street or you volunteer to serve in the soup kitchen in order to impress your friends. Or maybe you want to earn a merit badge so you can mention it on your college application. No matter, the rabbis would say. You did the deed. The blind person got across the street safely, the homeless person got fed. The deed is what counts. You fulfilled your obligation.

But even if intentionality is not required (and in the ritual sphere, especially regarding prayer, it usually is), walking the path is an outer expression of what is in the heart. It stems from a sense of commandment; that implies a relationship between the One Who commands and the one who responds. In fact the Hasidic authors, only half playfully, derive the Hebrew term *mitzvah*, or "commandment," not from the root meaning to command, but rather from an Aramaic word that means "to be" or "to work together." The *mitzvah*, including the halakhic way of performing it, is a deed in which God and the Jew are joined, an act in which we meet God.[4] It is an expression of the covenant; a declaration of love, loyalty, and commitment; an opportunity to encounter God's presence. That is much more than law. These same authors talk about *halakhah* as a way of walking toward God.

Because the Jewish community defined itself around patterns of behavior, it did not need to define itself by spelling out all the norms of theological orthodoxy. We are a community constituted more around what you *do* than what you *believe*. This leaves a lot of room for divergence of belief within the Jewish community, although certain broad parameters are understood to be taken for granted. This liberty included ways of understanding the commandments and their performance. Jews who do the same things and thus look alike from the outside may in fact have very different spiritual lives. A large body of literature developed alongside the *halakhah* that delves

into the meanings of the commandments. Here philoso-
phers and mystics were free to diverge on the most basic
issues of religious teaching, even though they observed
in almost exactly the same way and could sit next to one
another in the synagogue.

The same is true in our own day, when Hasidic or
neo-Hasidic Jews may think of a deed as an active token
of God's love, whereas the strict legalist, even if not really
sure about God, may live out the same pattern of deeds
because they are prescribed by the *Shulḥan 'Arukh*, or
"The Set Table," the operative code of Jewish practice.
Someone else might claim to be doing them just because
they are Jewish folkways, traditional forms that are fun
to observe. But who, indeed, knows what is within the
human heart? The devotion of the seemingly legalistic
person may be no less than that of the self-conscious
pietist. A Jew who thinks the *mitzvah* is just a nice custom may have a heart full of love and joy when doing it.

Those of us, myself included, who live outside what
is today called Jewish Orthodoxy, are selective when it
comes to *halakhah*. Both as individuals and communities,
we make our own choices about which areas of *halakhah*
still bind us and which do not. The practices around our
sacred calendar still have wide appeal, as do certain areas
of the life cycle, including those connected to death and

mourning. Many of us observe some degree of *kashrut*, or Jewish food restrictions, but few of us bother about matters of ritual impurity, a major concern of biblical and rabbinic *halakhah*. Almost none of us (including many self-defined as Orthodox) have our clothing checked to see that we avoid the Torah's ban of wearing a mixture of wool and linen. Why is that, and what is the point of observing some, but not all, of the traditions?

Such liberal Jews (to choose a term not linked with any particular denomination) may be expressing the same range of emotions and commitments that one finds among the more fully observant. Some believe that compromises are necessary for living in the modern world, where Jews rejoice in being part of an open society and do not wish to wall themselves off entirely into a voluntary ghetto. Practices that discourage or limit social interaction with others, for example, are set aside for the sake of an opposing value. Such prohibitions as drinking wine with non-Jews or eating food, even of kosher ingredients, cooked by non-Jews, seem unreasonable in our cultural setting. Others are more critical of the halakhic process itself, feeling that too much has been spelled out by rabbinic authorities over the centuries, that the norms of praxis are overly invasive of personal liberty, and that excessive concern for halakhic detail can take on a quality of obsessiveness that blocks the very freedom we need in order to open our hearts and express that which lies within them. Here there may arise a deep tension between a love of tradition and the pursuit of one's own spiritual path. Much of this has to do with personal history and psychological makeup.

Nearly all religious Jews seem to agree, however, that some degree of normative behavior (sometimes called "a" *halakhah*, if not "the" *halakhah*) is required for the ongoing life of the Jewish community. In this context, the changing fate of particular observances is most interesting to watch. The lighting of Hanukkah candles, publicly as well as privately, is much more widely observed among Jews today than it was fifty or a hundred years ago. This certainly has to do with the "December dilemma," as it is called, and the influence of the general non-Jewish culture. But so what? Another observance, that of the fifteenth day of the month of Shevat, or Tu bi-Shevat, is growing rapidly because of its reassignment as a day of Jewish environmental awareness. The *mikveh*, or ritual bath, once an object of mockery among the non-Orthodox, is being redefined and filled with the fresh water of new meaning in our day by some, both women and men. The *halakhah* that will become normative for liberal Jews in our society is still very much in the making. But the fact that Judaism is a religion of doers, requiring an active commitment, and that participation will be defined by deeds, will be with us for a long time to come.

# 4

# *TIKKUN 'OLAM*
## Repairing the World
### Being God's Partner

*T*ikkun *'olam*, which literally means mending or repairing the world, is an ancient Hebrew phrase that has taken on new meaning in recent decades. It originally meant something like "to establish the world as the kingdom of the Almighty," or to bring about God's rule on earth. In contemporary usage it refers to the betterment of the world: relieving human suffering, achieving peace and mutual respect among individuals and peoples, and protecting the planet itself from destruction.

In order to mend or repair something, you first have to acknowledge that it is broken. *Tikkun 'olam* begins with recognizing that we live in a broken world. This brokenness is most easily manifest to us in what we call the political realm. Bad regimes repress their people; ethnic and economic rivalries lead to hostility and even war; and people become divided across lines of class, race, and creed. All these are real problems that must be dealt with, but our world's brokenness goes much deeper. We do not ask ourselves what it means to be a human being, what we are doing in this world, or how we are to live out the gift of our lives. When we look at ourselves from the perspective of our very best moments, we know that we are not the people we could be or truly want to be. In our rush to survive, accomplish, and excel, all of which seem to run together at an ever faster pace, we have forgotten what it means to live in God's world, to celebrate the sacredness of life itself.

This story goes all the way back to Eden, the origin of our universal sense of exile or alienation. The opening tale of human life in our Torah has been interpreted in many ways by both Jewish and Christian readers. Some see it primarily as a story of human sinfulness or temptation. Others read it as a parable about the enchanted garden of childhood that has to break apart when we disobey the commanding parent. I see it as a myth about alienation—the distance between ourselves and God, but also between us and our truest selves. The ancient Jewish mystics said that we were expelled from Eden not for eating from the Tree of Knowledge, but for separating the Tree of Knowledge from the Tree of Life. We use knowledge for our own ends in a way that makes the natural world an *other*, an object to be conquered, rather than the home of which we are fully a part. We thus violate the original harmony of being, a primal oneness of life that waits to be rediscovered. This is the most essential tear in the fabric of life that needs to be mended. That is why environmental concerns are so central to *tikkun 'olam*; the original break is that between us and the world around us. All the rest of the fixing that needs to be done within the human community resides within that context. The repair of this original harmony is the very deepest of deep ecologies.

Rabbi Elimelekh and Reb Zusha were two brothers who together became disciples of the Rabbi of Mezritch (in late eighteenth-century Ukraine). Elimelekh was an intellectual, eventually the author of a major book of teachings. Zusha was more simple, but a wholly devoted servant of God's will. One day Elimelekh turned to his brother and said, "I just don't understand it! We are taught that every soul that was ever to be born was present in the soul of Adam. That means you and I were there, too. But such a holy person as you, how could you have let it happen? Why didn't you stop him from eating?" Zusha replied, "I saw it, and I knew what would happen; I saw that exile would result if he—or 'we'—ate of that tree. But I also knew that if he didn't eat it, we would have gone on through all of history exclaiming, 'Why didn't I eat it? If only I had eaten it!' So I had no choice."[1]

Ever since we bit into that fruit (again, proverbially rather than literally), we have lived in a broken world, and it is our human task to fix it. That is what we are here to do; all the rest is incidental. Our most basic moral message, that every human being embodies the divine image, demands that we be concerned with each person's welfare, including food, shelter, and health, and pursuit of a meaningful life. The Torah's call that we "pursue justice, justice" (Deut. 16:20) urges us to work toward closing the terrible gaps, especially in learning and opportunity, that mark our society. Even with this effort, we remain painfully aware that the relative wealth and comfort that we "developed world" inhabitants enjoy is too easily identified as the result of *'oshek*, "oppression," the taking of an unfair share of resources at the expense of others. As participants in the wealthiest of human societies, we are more than bystanders to the burdens suffered by the majority of people on our planet. We are also participants in the wanton destruction of forests, animal species, and much more. Living a life committed to *tikkun* as *restoration* demands a great deal of us.

The interesting evolution of *tikkun 'olam* has to do with the question of who is to bring about this repair of the world. In its original context, the bringer of *tikkun 'olam* is God, in whom we are to place our hope for a redeemed world. But the modern usage places humans as the responsible actors, the ones who need to usher in this world of justice. How did such a change take place? Most surprising is that it was the mystics, or Kabbalists, seemingly the most otherworldly of Jews, who brought about this transformation, seeing themselves as constantly engaged in repairing the universe. Where did they get the audacity to proclaim such an idea? The truth is that the view of life as a divine-human partnership has deep roots within the tradition, going back to our most ancient sources. The account of creation in Genesis reaches its climax when God sanctifies the Sabbath. That passage ends with a verse that says, if read literally, "God blessed the seventh day and made it holy, for in it God rested from all the labor that God created *to do*" (Gen. 2:3). The "to do" of that verse was taken to mean that God's creation was left incomplete; there remains an essential task left up to humans, that human action is required to fulfill creation's purpose.

God puts humans in the garden "to work it and guard it" (Gen. 2:15). This is taken to refer to the essential sense of human life as fulfilling the divine command. When God calls out, "Where are you?" in response to Adam's sin (Gen. 3:9), all future human generations are somehow being called to account. "Where are you" in fulfilling God's purpose in creation? Rephrased in our contemporary understanding of human origins, this might sound like "Where are you in fulfilling the best of your evolutionary legacy? Where are you in being human in the fullest sense of that word, bearing within you the image of the divine? Are you living and acting that way? The universe needs you to do so. Without that, your planet may not be able to survive!"

Then what about the messiah? If we are here to repair the world, what do God and the messiah do at the end of time? The Kabbalists, we should remember, were firm believers in the messiah and spawned some rather vigorous messianic movements. They believed that all of our *tikkun 'olam* was preparation for the final and most dangerous tasks. We could uplift all the broken fragments, reignite all the lost sparks of light (to use another of their favorite symbols) except the very darkest ones. The messiah would come to take care of those. But the messiah could come to do that task only when we had nearly completed our own, the one we carried through history: redeeming the cosmos bit by bit.

To be a Jew is to remain committed to doing that work. Even highly secularized Jews in the last two centuries took much of this value system as their own, while either denying or remaining unaware of its source. Ultimately, of course, it goes back to the prophets, who were revolutionaries in their own way. Imbued with the word of God, they challenged the societies in which they lived. They denounced false religion and repression of the poor and needy as two faces of the same turning away from God. Sometimes they brought forth images of violence in calling for the overthrow of the unjust old order. Their words are not easy to read or understand, and we cannot simply substitute their very specific historical context for our own. Nevertheless, their words retain great power and make an uncompromising demand on the way we live.

The notion that we are here to do God's work, treating those in need with decency and justice, remains essential to our faith. It is our task to fix the broken world, to get it ready for a messianic era that is still to come. The dream of an earthly era when all will live together in the harmony of a restored Eden is a dream that has never left us.

# 5

# SHABBAT

## Getting Off
## the Treadmill

### The Secret of Shabbat

I am the Jew I am today largely because of my close relationship with my mother's parents, immigrant Jews who had been brought up in the premodern world of small-town Eastern Europe and who came to America in the early years of the twentieth century. They were not what one would call Orthodox Jews; Grandpa's tailor shop was open on Saturdays, although he regretted it. Grandma, in their apartment over the store, ran a tighter ship. There was no cooking on the Sabbath, no writing, and no sewing. Her home was strictly kosher.

But could you really keep kosher in America? It wasn't like the old country, she would complain, where you knew who slaughtered each chicken, who plucked the feathers, and everything else about it. You should investigate, she said, and find out if the butcher is *shomer Shabbat* (or *Shabbos*, as she would have pronounced it), a strict Sabbath observer. If he is, she said, you can trust his meat. Otherwise, beware. America is a pretty corrupt and dangerous place.

How did observing the Sabbath become the defining trait of a citizen in good standing in the world of Jewish piety? Why not some other commandment, such as that of daily prayer, of giving to the poor, or even of believing in God and the Torah? Why is it a Sabbath observer who may be trusted, serving as a proper witness on a Jewish legal document, for example?

We don't have an answer to that question, but we do have a good story about it. Rabbi Elisha ben Abuya is one of the great sages in the early second century, another friend of Rabbi Akiva. His chief disciple was Meir, who was to become a major teacher in his own right. But something happened to Elisha. He rejected the way of the rabbis, followed some other teaching (we're not sure which) and departed from the rabbinic form of obser-vance. Still, Meir respected his knowledge and wanted to learn from him. One Sabbath day, after Elisha's apostasy, they were walking together outside town and discussing Torah. When they were two thousand cubits (about one thousand yards) from the town's edge, Elisha said to his disciple, "Go back!" for only thus far is one allowed to walk outside the town on the Sabbath. To step beyond it was to leave behind the observant community. Even though Elisha no longer observed the rule, he still knew it and was concerned for his disciple. Meir turned to his teacher and said, meaning much more than geography, "You too come back!" But Elisha could not, and the two men parted ways.[1] Here we see the border of Jewish life being drawn: to stand inside it is to live within the Sabbath rules, to walk farther is to go outside the bounds of traditional Jewish life and the community of those who observe it.

For many Jews entering the modern world, it all seemed so old-fashioned and repressive. The Sabbath was just a great list of "don'ts." For Americans, these looked too much like the old blue laws, unwelcome restrictions on our inalienable right to "pursue happiness" by drinking and shopping seven days a week. Whole generations of Jews rebelled against the Sabbath laws, until their observance became the exception rather than the norm.

But today we look at Shabbat from a different, more contemporary, perspective. We are living through one of the great ages of the speeding up of human consciousness. How incredibly fast the pace of our lives has become! The computer revolution, and with it the possibility of virtually instantaneous worldwide communication, has made us think about time in new terms. How many times a day do you check your email? How soon do people expect you to respond to their queries and messages? Remember when letters used to take two or three days to arrive? "Snail mail," we call it now. Just watch your child playing computer games and see how fast that fleeting object runs across the screen. Could we chase *anything* that fast a generation ago? We worry about the effect all this may have on the human mind.

What has happened to our leisure? Remember all those labor-saving devices, all those prepackaged foods and household gadgets that were supposed to save us so much time? Where has that free time gone? It seems as though it's all been a plot just to free us up to work harder than ever, to answer messages ever faster, to squeeze more productivity out of each minute of our lives.

Shabbat is needed now more than ever. We Jews should be *missionary* about Shabbat. It may be the best gift we have to offer the world. The idea is that one day a week you say no to our new master, the computer. You turn off the modem, look away from the screen and toward those around you, exercising a talent that may become rare in this age: the cultivation of real human community. My bumper-sticker slogan for Shabbat reads "Visit people, not websites."

But in order to give Shabbat to the world, we first need to reclaim it for ourselves. Most Jews, in the rush toward modernity, lost the rhythms of Shabbat and need to rediscover them. Shabbat does not belong only to the Orthodox minority who observe it strictly; it is the inheritance of all Jews. But how shall we do it? What might constitute a contemporary Shabbat?

Before we get to the specifics, we need to understand something about how the Shabbat rules came to be. Shabbat is made holy, or set aside from others days, according to the Torah, at the creation of the world. "God rested on the seventh day and hallowed it" (Gen. 2:3). I believe this is the Torah's way of saying that human life is not even *conceivable* without a day of rest; it was there from the very beginning. Unlike in ancient Near Eastern religions, where humans were created as servants, destined to bring offerings so that the gods could rest, here human beings are invited to partake of the divine gift of leisure. Not just the king or the upper classes were given the commandment of leisure, but everyone, "so that your manservant and maidservant rest *as you do*" (Deut. 5:14). And we rest as God does.

But how do we define that leisure? The Torah, while emphasizing its importance, is remarkably sparing in detail. The only rules provided, beyond "you shall do no labor," are prohibitions on gathering wood and lighting a fire. (Of course, that tells us a lot about the age from which these rules come.) In sharp contrast to Shabbat, however, the Torah happens to blossom with detail on another matter: how to create a portable ark and a tabernacle for God's presence. Four full weekly Torah sections are devoted to spelling out those details! Unfortunately, however, all that information has become useless. Once built, the tabernacle of Moses was never to be created again.

Here enters a bit of rabbinic genius. "If words of Torah are spare in one place," we are taught, "they are rich in another."[2] If the matter is useless here, use it over there. So the sages enumerated thirty-nine categories of work that were required to construct the tabernacle: sawing wood, dying cloth, and all the rest. These thirty-nine labors (the term *mel'akhah*, or "labor," is used in both contexts), they said, turned around to the negative, are those prohibited on the Sabbath.

On what basis could they make such a claim? You could say that they found a *but*. One passage describing the tabernacle is interrupted with "*but* you shall keep my Sabbaths" (Exod. 31:13). This is taken to mean that the work of construction, in all its parts, was to pause in honor of the Sabbath. But did they really build the whole edifice of Sabbath law on that one word? The Talmud itself refers to the emerging Sabbath laws as "mountains hanging by a hair"[3] in their weak connection to any mandate found in Scripture.

Something else is going on here. The rabbis understood that all holiness comes from God, the One Who cannot be limited by either space or time. Y-H-W-H is the place of the world, filling all of the earth with glory yet remaining entirely elusive. God existed before the world came to be and will exist afterward, when all is ended. Yet that One comes to be manifest in both the spatial and temporal realms. All the rules are given for constructing sacred space. Very well, said the rabbis, those same rules turned around backward, prohibited instead of prescribed, tell us how to construct sacred time. The Sabbath, in Rabbi Heschel's words, is "a palace in time." Of course it is to be constructed like God's little palace on earth, with the same set of rules.

Shabbat thus becomes a mirror image of the tabernacle or the later Temple. In the age after the Temple was destroyed, Jews made Shabbat the key defining form of

Jewish religious life. Because it was replacing the Temple, it had to look like it. Indeed, the conversation between Elisha and Meir took place in that age, just when the rules were being firmly set.

Today our needs are different and I believe that Shabbat has to take on forms appropriate to our age. Although many of the old thirty-nine categories are still useful, I offer here a simplified Shabbat for moderns: ten rules—five positive and five prohibitions. This numbering is based, of course, on the form of the ten commandments.

Try these out. Add them to your own Shabbat, whatever it currently is. See which ones work for you. Welcome others, Jews and non-Jews, to try them on for size. Be a Shabbat missionary. The world will one day thank us for it.

## Ten Pathways toward a New Shabbat

### Do

1. Stay at home. Spend quality time with family and real friends.
2. Celebrate with others: at the table, in the synagogue, with friends or community.

3. Study or read something that will edify, challenge, or make you grow.

4. Be alone. Take some time for yourself. Check in with yourself. Review your week. Ask yourself where you are in your life.

5. Mark the beginning and end of this sacred time by lighting candles and making *kiddush* on Friday night and saying *havdalah* on Saturday night.

## Don't

6. Don't do anything you have to do for your work life. This includes obligatory reading, homework for kids (even without writing!), unwanted social obligations, and preparing for work as well as doing your job itself.

7. Don't spend money. Separate completely from the commercial culture that surrounds us so much. This includes doing business of all sorts. No calls to the broker, no following up on ads, no paying of bills. It can all wait.

8. Don't use the computer. Turn off the iPhone or smartphone or whatever device has replaced it by the time you read this. Live and breathe for a day without checking messages. Declare your freedom

from this new master of our minds and our time. Find the time for face-to-face conversations with people around you, without Facebook.

9. Don't travel. Avoid especially commercial travel and places like airports, hotel check-ins, and similar depersonalizing encounters. Stay free of situations in which people are likely to tell you to "have a nice day" (Shabbat already *is* a nice day, thank you).

10. Don't rely on commercial or canned video entertainment, including the TV as well as the computer screen. Discover what there is to do in life when you are not being entertained.

# TESHUVAH

## Returning

### Faith in Human Change

**A** few years ago I had the privilege of serving as Hebrew text editor of a new Jewish prayer book. Working with committees, both rabbinic and lay, on the question of what should be included, led to some fascinating conversations. One concerned the second section of the daily recited *Shema'*, actually a passage from the Torah (Deut. 11:13–21). The passage is all about reward and punishment, the worldly bounty that would result from loving God and being faithful to His word and a warning of the dangers of arousing God's anger if one transgressed His will.

The committee members were certain they did not want this passage in their prayer book. It seemed so juvenile, so much the "good and bad parent" religion they had fled, so guilt producing. "Spare the rod and spoil the child" was hardly the way they were raising their own next generation, and they certainly didn't want to think of God as still living by that outdated slogan. But then someone in the group suggested removing the personal metaphor from the passage in question. "What is this passage teaching?" he asked. "Deeds have consequences. We are responsible for the outcome of the way we live." He applied it especially to ecological questions, since the passage spoke of God bringing or withholding rain. "Oh," people replied, "you mean *karma. Of course* we believe in karma. Our deeds affect our fate and that of those around us, and we have to act responsibly." The passage was included.

This little vignette reveals much about the current state of the Jewish faith. But what interests me here is that both the frightening angry God version and the depersonalized "law of karma," adapted from the Hindu tradition, are teaching the same lesson: there is an inexorable connection between deeds, especially in the realm of morality, and the results they bring about. Judaism no longer believes that in the most direct and literal sense, even though some of our oldest sources proclaim it. The connection between deed and outcome may be broken in the sense that there is no *inevitable* result. That is because of a great innovation in the realm of moral thinking wrought by the prophets of Israel: the idea of *teshuvah*, repentance or return to God.

The earliest prophetic writings in the Bible contain no evidence of this idea. God's covenant means that Israel bears an extra measure of responsibility for its deeds. If Israel has sinned, it will surely be punished. Prepare for the outpouring of God's wrath! But by the time you get to the later prophets, those of the Second Temple period, the compassionate God offers a hand outstretched to all who would return to Him. "You do not desire that the sinner die," as a later formula has it, "but rather that he return from his [or her] wicked ways and live."[1] What stands between these two bodies of prophecies is one of the most remarkable little stories ever written: the book of Jonah.

Jonah, you may recall, is sent by God to prophesy against Nineveh, a great, wicked, pagan city. Jonah runs away from his task and tries to flee to Tarshish, the other end of the known world. It takes a whale of a story, you might say, to bring him back to where he is supposed to go. He chose to flee, he tells God later, because he has a cynical view of human nature. He understands that the people will become greatly afraid when he prophesies destruction. They will don sackcloth and ashes and go about weeping to God to forgive their sins. God in His compassion will do just that. "But the Lord is too soft-hearted!" Jonah protests. No real transformation will take place in the Ninevites' hearts. People are good actors, but they don't really change. Soon they will be back to their wicked ways. That's the way humans are.

The book is about the moral education of the prophet. God sends the whale not only to protect Jonah but to set him back on his course. Even if Jonah does not believe real change is possible in the human heart, God does. The One Who made us and gave us free will also takes the remarkable risk of *trusting* us, of betting on the faith that human beings really are capable of sincere and lasting change. God puts His faith in the people of Nineveh, teaching and admonishing Jonah to learn to do the same.

We read the book of Jonah every year just before the dramatic conclusion of our daylong Yom Kippur service. For a period of forty days we have been called upon to reconsider our lives, examine our deeds, and return to God. There are many reasons that journey is a difficult one. The forces to be overcome—greed, selfishness, insecurity, and all the rest—are just too powerful. Sometimes these urges have led us into complicated situations from which it is genuinely difficult to become extricated. But often we just don't have sufficient faith in ourselves, in our own ability to grow or change. This lack of self-trust often gets hidden behind a mask of cynicism. But then, in this last dramatic moment, the divine voice, now speaking through the prophet, calls out, "But *I* believe in you. I, the One Who made you, know you better than you know yourself. I can see the goodness that lies within you. I know you can be a better person than you dare to admit, even to yourself." Put like that, the call is hard to resist.

Although the *idea* of *teshuvah* may have originated in history, the mystics view it as eternal, essential to the world's existence. The Talmud includes it as part of a mysterious list of seven things that came to be even before the world was created, meaning that human life itself is inconceivable without the possibility of return to God or restoring one's lost inner balance. The first humans sought *teshuvah* after being expelled from the Garden of Eden.[2] *Teshuvah* in this case would mean reestablishing the intimacy and trust between God and these beings He created out of love. It could not mean a return to the innocence of Eden, which indeed was gone forever, just as childhood must come to an end as we grow into maturity. But a new relationship, which has faced and bridged over the deep chasms of betrayal, doubt, and anger, can now grow into a profound loving faith. This is the religion of adults, forged out of a mature understanding of *teshuvah*.

If there is a notion of "original sin" in the rabbinic tradition, it is much more likely that of the Golden Calf than that of our first parents' sexual awareness. While Moses was still on the mountaintop receiving God's Torah, Israel was busy making and worshipping an idol. We are too easily swayed, drawn after false gods. These are as present in our own society of Hollywood idols, sports icons, and the pursuit of success and money as they were in the days of Ba'al and Molekh. God was so fed up with the Israelites when they worshipped the Golden Calf that He was ready to destroy them, to unleash the "nuclear option."

The Torah's "holy of holies," you might say, occurs at this moment. As Moses prays and argues for the Israelites' forgiveness (Exod. 34), the most famous of all texts describing God is spoken by a mysterious divine voice:

> Y-H-W-H, Y-H-W-H, a compassionate and gracious God, long-suffering and magnanimous in true love, keeping that love for the multitudes, forgiving sin, transgression, and misdeed, but surely not cleansing

them entirely, revisiting the sins of the fathers upon their children, down to the third and fourth generations. (Exod. 34:6–7)

The early synagogue adopted this passage as central to its liturgy. To this day, all penitential prayers are built around it as a refrain. It is central to the Yom Kippur service. But when read in the synagogue, the text is rather different:

Y-H-W-H, Y-H-W-H, a compassionate and gracious God, long-suffering and magnanimous in true love, keeping that love for the multitudes, forgiving sin, transgression, and misdeed, and cleansing!

The absolute form of the verb *naqeh* ("cleansing") is simply cut off from the negative it was meant to underscore, with its meaning totally transformed. The whole latter part of the verse where God "revisits the sins" and punishes later generations has disappeared. This is a total reversal of the text; it documents like no other source the transformation of God as One Who seeks retribution from descendants of uncleansed sinners into One Who forgives and cleanses with unmitigated compassion. Judaism, it turns out, does *not* believe in karma. It believes in the possibility of wiping the slate clean and starting over.

Other voices within the tradition understand the claim of primordial *teshuvah* to mean that our human longing to return to our Source is fully part of the natural order. We are born to be God-seekers. The soul quests after God in the same way that trees grow in the direction of sunlight, pulled by an inner force that tells them to reach out toward what they need, to attain their nourishment. Their very lives depend upon their ability to respond to this inward call. "As the deer pants after streams of water, so does my soul long for You" (Ps. 42:2).

*Teshuvah* belongs not only to our encounter with God but also to the interpersonal realm. For harm done to another person, repenting to God does not suffice. Even the great cleansing power of Yom Kippur, we are told, is ineffective in wiping away transgressions against another person until we have reconciled with the one we have harmed.[3] This is the harder part of *teshuvah*, because it demands that we make ourselves contrite and vulnerable before someone who may or may not be ready to forgive. We trust that God accepts our contrition, but with humans we are less sure. When we stand on the other side of the equation and are asked to forgive, we know that we are supposed to respond with an open heart, even though that too may not be easy. We do so in the hope that when the situation is reversed, our own *teshuvah* will find acceptance as well.

# TORAH

## The People
## and the Book

### Text and Interpretation

Judaism is a civilization built around a text. That text is called the Torah, or the "Teaching," and consists of the five books of Moses, the first section of the Hebrew Bible. Although historians believe the Torah text as we have it was canonized by Ezra and his followers around the fifth century Before the Common Era, the Jewish imagination sees it all as having happened at Mount Sinai, that mysterious encounter in the wilderness where Israel collectively said "Yes!" to each of God's commandments even before it was given and God handed us the Torah as a token of our covenant and love.

Whenever the final text came into being, the process of interpretation was already going on before that. If you hold strictly to the Sinai view, you may find yourself saying that Moses in his old age, when he was making those great speeches before his death that constitute the book of Deuteronomy, was already revising through commentary some things he had said, or even heard from God, earlier in his life. If you follow the historians, it is clear that the Torah text stands in dialogue with prophetic and other writings of ancient Israel and that these often comment on and respond to one another.

But the process of commentary really gets going later in the Second Temple period (beginning around 150 BCE), when new revelations were no longer accepted. (Yes, that's the right word. There were still people who thought they heard God speaking, but the community stopped listening.) As the Romans ruled Judea, each group among the Judean populace thought they had a proper understanding of God's word: the priests, the Pharisees, the extreme pietists who retreated to the Dead Sea, and the small nascent Christian community. The rabbis, heirs to the Pharisees, saw Torah study and the process of commentary as the highest ideals of Jewish life. Once the Temple was destroyed in 70 CE, the life of Torah became the new sacred center around which all of Judaism revolved.

The most famous story of that early era tells of a dispute between Rabbi Eliezer and the sages, on a fine point of emerging Jewish practice revolving around the ritual purity of a certain type of oven. All the rational arguments possible were exhausted, but the two sides could not agree. Then heaven seemed to intervene on the side of Rabbi Eliezer: a tree leaned sideways, a brook flowed backward. Finally a heavenly voice came forth and took his side. The majority view was that of Rabbi Joshua, who, quoting the Torah itself, proclaimed, "It is not in heaven" (Deut. 30:12). The Torah has already been given; its interpretation is in human hands, not God's. A talmudic postscript to the story adds: "What was God doing at that moment? Smiling and saying: 'My children have defeated Me! My children have defeated Me!'"[1]

Freedom of interpretation became the lifeblood of Jewish creativity. Sometimes it was very daring, uprooting clear commandments of the Torah that seemed heartless to a later, more compassionate age. Deuteronomy 21:18–21 says that a rebellious and gluttonous son may be stoned to death. The rabbis, clearly quite horrified by this dictum, proclaimed that there had never been such an execution. The following chapter calls for the same penalty for a rape victim if she was betrothed to another man. If the incident took place within a city and she did not cry out, she is presumed to share in the liability, and she is put to death along with her attacker (Deut. 22:23–24). Such are called "honor killings" in some parts of the world. Yes, the Torah prescribes them, but we have no record of post-biblical Jews ever carrying them out. Indeed the death penalty itself was anathema to some of the early sages. They proclaimed that any high court that found one person in seven—and some said seventy!—years liable to execution should be considered a court of murderers.[2]

How could they dare to make such changes, if Torah was the will of God? They did it in the presence of that smiling Deity, the One Who wanted His children to win the argument. Might this be a personified way of talking about tradition's evolution? The One Who set it in motion, dwelling beyond space and time, knows that Torah will have to be carried forward, brought up-to-date, not only regarding technological advances (ranging all the way from "Can you open that refrigerator on the Sabbath?" to "Is cloning kosher?") but also regarding evolving moral perspectives.

This process of creative rereading or intentional misreading of the Torah is called Midrash, meaning "inquiry" or "deep search" into the text. It involves a whole complex of interpretive strategies, using various tools of juxtaposition, cross-reading, typologies, acronyms, and more, all seeking to reveal new facets of each word and letter of Torah. Often the midrashic sources will offer multiple interpretations of a single verse, presenting each of them as a legitimate reading: *davar aher*—another reading—and then yet another, all lined up in a row. Torah is true, the Word of God, but it is expansive enough to embrace all these meanings. Judaism has always been a tradition of faithfulness to our sacred texts, but it has never been fundamentalist in terms of how to read them.

One day I was leaving my house to teach a class of rabbinical students. On the way to my car, I noticed a pickup truck parked nearby with a bumper sticker that read, *God said it. I believe it. That settles it.* I walked into my class and told the students about it. "That," I said, "is not a Jewish bumper sticker! Our bumper sticker (even a strictly Orthodox one, by the way) would read clearly, *God said it. I believe it. Now let's talk about what it means....*"

The Kabbalists, medieval Spanish Jewish mystics, influenced by images of chivalry, depict the interpreter as a male lover of Torah, which is a beautiful maiden dwelling in a high tower.[3] Knowing how much he loves her, she reveals a bit more of her face to him each time he seeks her out. Interpretation of Torah becomes a sort of seduction. We picture the mystic singing and strumming his interpretive "guitar" beneath her window as she pulls the curtains farther open. The metaphor has to be read carefully. Rather than our working the cold magic of literary criticism onto a passive text, we are here engaged in an act of love with a living partner, drawing both "her," the Torah, and ourselves into ever greater bonds of intimacy by this ongoing quest for deeper meanings within the text. We seek her out and court her, but it is she who opens her secrets before us.

That's a key point. Interpretation opens and widens the text, allows us to find ourselves within it, to make room within tradition for our own unique perspective. But it also affirms the text; we make Torah our own as we find ourselves within it. As we work to interpret the text, we have a chance to reshape it in our own image. But as long as we are busy reading and engaging with the sources, Torah has the power to reshape *us* as well.

A Jew who is called forth to partake in the synagogue's Torah service recites after each portion of the text that is read, "Blessed are You … Who *has given* us the Torah of truth and implanted eternal life within us. Blessed are You, Y-H-W-H, Who *gives* the Torah." Listen to a Hasidic reading of this blessing: The Torah, given once to the ancients (hence the past tense of "has given"), can become the "Torah of truth" only when each reader takes that "eternal life" implanted within us and uses it to reread Torah in a way that speaks to his or her own life. We make Torah come to life. Only then are we able to say that God "gives" the Torah, right now, in the present moment.[4] God not only resides behind the text as guarantor of its infinite elasticity but also dwells *within us*, in the innermost chambers of our endless creativity.

We, together with God, bring life to Torah and Torah to life.

# TALMUD TORAH

תלמוד תורה

## "Teach Them to Your Children"

### The Role of Education

If you were to ask me what single precept of Judaism is the one to which Jews feel the greatest commitment, I could answer completely without hesitation. "You shall teach them diligently to your children" (Deut. 6:7): the commandment to educate, to pass the legacy of tradition and its knowledge onward from generation to generation. Jews have a particularly strong awareness that our lives serve as bridges between those who came before and those who will come after us; each of us is a living link between our grandparents and our grandchildren. Even in families where the thick and rich stew of that heritage has become so watered down as to be almost tasteless, Jews still feel an obligation to "pass it on," while hardly knowing what the "it" is. Ask any non-Orthodox American rabbi why most Jews join his or her synagogue; the answer will be clear. People say, "I want my son to know he's Jewish, to be proud of his heritage." Or today, even more pointedly, "We want our daughter to share in the knowledge that for so long belonged only to men," but for the same purpose, "to understand what it means to be a Jew," something she too will give to her children, thus passing on the torch.

The commitment to learning as the chief vehicle of continuity is not something that is immediately obvious. In most traditional societies it was the land itself, especially agricultural land, that constituted the patrimony to be handed down. There are parts of the world where ancient enmities and memories of tribal conflict are the stuff of legacy. Jews certainly have these memories as well. But beginning more than two millennia ago, the Jewish people identified its culture as one of Torah, literally meaning "teaching," and knowledge became the essential tool for participation in that culture, passed on from each generation to the next. Jewish heroes over the course of those centuries include very few warriors or statesmen, only a handful of artists, and not many people of special physical prowess or athletic ability, but a great many scholars and sages. To be a *ben Torah*, a person of learning, was the aspiration that Jewish society valued most.

For much of that long period, this knowledge was largely internal: sacred texts, commentaries, legal compilations, codes, works of philosophy, and mystic lore written by Jews and intended for consumption within the Jewish community. The apex in this culture of learning was the Talmud, the vast compilation of law and lore completed by the rabbis of Babylonia in about the sixth century CE. The complex dialectics of talmudic argumentation, especially in the legal sections, became the paradigm for a typical style of Jewish thinking that spread over the ages and through the world. (Much of Jewish humor, by the way, is an imitation and parody of that style of discourse.) A special institution was created for intellectual conversation in the dialectical mode. The *hevruta* or study partnership, in which two people ask each other questions, demolish each other's arguments, and help clarify and reframe their thinking, is a particularly Jewish form of friendship. It is carried on in the *bet midrash*, or house of study, a communal learning hall that in traditional communities stands alongside the synagogue as a key communal institution.

This valuing of intellectual achievement worked well as a tool for Jewish survival through the long period of exile and diaspora. The spread of knowledge went from great feats of oral memorization to the copying of manuscripts and then to the wonder of printed books. These meant that one could engage in a conversation (long before the age of cyberspace) seated around a virtual *bet midrash* table with two disputing sages from second-century Galilee, an eleventh-century French commentator, a sixteenth-century Turkish codifier, a nineteenth-century Polish questioner, and one's own study partner. The wisdom of tradition was always seen as cumulative, each generation of students and scholars standing on the shoulders of all those who had come before.

As Jews entered the modern world, beginning in the late eighteenth century, their faith and accrued skills in textual reasoning came to be applied to new, broader realms of knowledge. The massive attraction of Jews to higher education, both in Europe and in contemporary America, is the result of a number of factors. Some of it is about the desire to get ahead in social and economic terms. When Jews were still seen as low-class outsiders in Western societies, we felt a need to try harder than anyone else in order to claim our place. The breakdown of the intellectual ghetto walls was also seen as a great liberation for many Jews who felt confined and constricted by the ancient rubrics of Jewish learning, most of which had little to do with the struggle to live in the contemporary world. The turn to modernity, we should add, also eventually gave educational opportunity to Jewish women, the 50 percent of the population that had been excluded from the world of traditional Jewish learning.

The new Jewish society that became the modern state of Israel was created by generations of so-called pioneers who believed that European Jews had become too intellectualized. They sought a world where Jews would be farmers and laborers rather than professors. This vision lasted for two or perhaps three generations, but it soon became clear that Israel's strength lay in the life of the mind. Although Israel's current educational system leaves much to be desired, the fact is that most farm and manual labor in today's Israel is done by Arab or international migrant workers, and the nation excels in high-tech, medical, and other learning-based innovations.

The academic community of North America over the course of the past half a century or more has been greatly enriched, even partly shaped, by the contribution of Jews far beyond our presence in the general population. Once the discriminatory quotas and "gentlemen's agreements" excluding us broke down, beginning in the early post-World War II years, both faculties and students, especially in the highest-ranking institutions, have embraced large Jewish populations.

For much of this period, Jews in the academy were one of the most secularized segments of the Jewish community. The first group to arrive at the universities consisted of children of immigrants, forged in Depression-era poverty and naturally attracted to the politics of the left, including a passion for social justice. Their vision of an ideal society was a thinly secularized version of the ancient Jewish prophetic dream, even if they did not recognize it as such. After them came Jews of my own generation, partly shaped by the great social changes of the 1960s. These and their successors, while more fully Americanized, disproportionately maintain a belief in the value of education, especially a sense that it bears responsibility for social transformation, including the eradication of inequality and poverty. In that sense, I would claim, some deep part of our ancient Jewish legacy has passed into the American mainstream.

But what of our own educational efforts, the attempt to pass on Jewish traditions to current generations of Jews? Jewish education in America is hardly a tale of unmitigated success. The afternoon Hebrew school was the bane of most Jewish kids' lives for much of the twentieth century. Valiant efforts by teachers, both professional and volunteer, could not overcome the fatigue and boredom of sitting still for another two hours after a long school day; the greater attractiveness of the general culture, including sports; and, perhaps most important, the readily perceived gap of practices taught in school but ignored in the home. Those same parents who strove so hard to get their kids to attend Hebrew School, at least until age thirteen and the great ritual reward moment, did rather little to witness to Judaism's importance in the lives of their children on a daily basis.

The ongoing achievements of Jews in secular learning alongside this widespread failure of Jewish supplementary education has led to an unacceptable disparity in American Jewish life between the levels of general intellectual sophistication and the mastery of even the most basic forms of Jewish knowledge. Jews who possess advanced degrees in the sciences or humanities or who are highly successful in law, medicine, or other education-based professions are often virtually illiterate when it comes to Judaism or Hebrew. This is often manifest by the embarrassment such people feel when receiving an honor in the synagogue, when trying to recite the blessing over Hanukkah candles, or when trying to conduct even the most basic sort of Passover seder. Many congregations now offer adult Jewish literacy classes to help overcome this chasm. Such classes are often of special importance to women, who were given no Jewish education in the era before the bat mitzvah was widely embraced as a significant Jewish rite (around 1980).

In the course of passing tradition from one generation to the next, it is important to note that the tradition carried forward has to be enriched and reshaped, not merely preserved, by its custodians in each generation. The Judaism my grandparents imbibed in small-town Eastern Europe would hardly be the proper vehicle for my grandchildren and their descendants in the fast-paced, open-ended, and culturally diverse America of tomorrow. If we look at the past few decades, these generational enrichments may be clearly seen. Enthusiasm over the new Jewish state, including modern Hebrew song and dance, were added in the 1950s and 1960s. These were followed in subsequent decades by the growth of Holocaust memory and the effort to liberate Soviet Jews. Then toward the turn of the new century came the full inclusion of women in Jewish life and emerging new perspectives brought about by it. Most recently, we note the reembracing of mysticism, meditation, and spiritual search as legitimate parts of Judaism. Each of these has successively served to enliven Jewish education for both youth and adults.

I have devoted much of my life to educating a leadership for American Jewry in the mid-twenty-first century, a generation of rabbis who will be able to provide contemporary and compelling answers to the question, "Why should we care? Why should we make the effort to pass this tradition forward from each generation to the next?" The answers vary, depending on both the person asking and the time in which it is asked. But seeking the answers throughout our lives is its own great reward.

# 9

# L'ḤAYYIM

## To Life!

### Accepting Death, Affirming Life

Latching on to a biblical phrase, the Talmud declares that God's commandments are given in such a way that one should "live by them" (Lev. 18:5), rather than die for them. Human life is considered sacred; saving a single life is like saving the entire world. Martyrdom is not to be sought and is to be accepted as one's fate only when there is truly no alternative. With few exceptions, all the commandments may be set aside for the sake of saving a human life. *We believe in life.* That means life in this world, in this body, with all its limitations.

Although the Jewish imagination freely depicts worlds other than our own—a divine throne room in a heaven full of angels, a realm of souls not yet born, a paradise to reward the righteous, and many more—all agree that the only place to serve God is here on earth, in this brief period when we live as fully embodied spirits. Although Judaism formally accepted a belief in the eternity of life, even including the future bodily resurrection of the dead, it never permitted the afterlife to become the centerpiece of Jewish faith. "Greater is one hour of fulfilling commandments and doing good in this world," says the Talmud, "than all the life of the World to Come."[1]

"Do not be like a servant who serves his master in order to receive a reward," teaches the Mishnah in tractate *Avot*, "but be rather like one who serves not in order to receive a reward."[2] A variant text, however, reads the latter section differently: "Be rather like one who serves *in order not* to receive a reward."

"What sort of service is that?" asks a later commentator. Who serves *in order not* to receive a reward? The king invites all his servants to come before him, he answers with a parable. Each one is assured that whatever he asks of the king will be granted immediately. But one faithful servant remains troubled. "All I want," he says, "is to be in the king's presence." As soon as I ask for it, my wish will be granted, and then I will be dismissed from that

presence."³ Such a servant lives the religious life *in order
not* to receive his reward. "One thing I ask of Y-H-W-H;
that is what I seek: to dwell in the house of Y-H-W-H all
the days of my life, to gaze upon the beauty of Y-H-W-H
and to visit His palace" (Ps. 27:4).

The famous preacher Dov Baer of Mezritch, later a
key figure in the founding of Hasidism, was in his youth
a humble teacher of children, barely earning a livelihood.
One Passover he and his wife faced the shame of complete poverty, having nothing in the house with which to
celebrate the festival. Dov Baer, wanting to trust only in
God, waited until late to leave the synagogue after evening prayers, for he did not want any of his neighbors,
seeing no lighted candles in his window, to invite him
and his family to join them for the Passover seder.

How surprised he was, approaching his house alone,
to see it bathed in light, a large carriage parked nearby.
He entered the house and saw a table set with all that was
needed for the holiday meal, and a well-dressed stranger
was waiting to be his guest. Overwhelmed with gratitude and joy, he immediately launched into the seder
and its tale of salvation from bondage without asking any
questions of his guest. When the time came for the meal
itself, again he was so filled with both joy and hunger
that he could not ask.

Finally, after they had eaten, he turned to his guest. "Who are you?" he inquired. "And what has brought you here?" The man explained that he was a wealthy estate agent from a nearby village, that he had heard of Dov Baer's growing reputation for saintliness, and had seen it as a privilege to spend this holy evening in his presence. Knowing the teacher was a poor man, he had brought along everything they would need.

"But what can I do to repay you?" asked the teacher. "I have no worldly goods, but is there no prayer or blessing I can offer you?"

"In fact," replied his guest, "my wife and I are childless. Perhaps you can pray to God that we conceive a child."

"God bless you," Dov Baer answered. "Next year this time you will have a child." They then proceeded to complete the seder.

Later that night, Dov Baer's wife awoke and saw that he was not in bed. She went into the front room where the seder had been conducted and saw him dancing around the table with a glow on his face that she had never seen before. "Berl," she called, using his Yiddish name. "What has happened? Why are you dancing like that?"

"I had a dream," he told her, "and a divine voice spoke to me. It told me that this man, because of some misdeed

in a former incarnation, had been fated to remain childless. But because I promised him a child, heaven decreed
that I could not be let down, and this couple will be
granted fertility. Because I forced the hand of heaven,
however, I am to have no portion in the World to Come."

His wife was devastated on hearing this news. "But
why all the dancing?" she asked in horror. "Why do you
look more radiant than ever before?"

"Don't you understand?" he told her. "Until now
I never trusted myself as God's servant. I always said,
'Yes, but you're doing it for the reward! Of course you're
doing good; you want a place in eternity!' Now that I
know I have no place in the World to Come, the slate is
clean. Now I can truly begin serving God!"[4]

Most Jews today are rather openly agnostic about
reward in the afterlife, causing them to cling even more
proudly to the message of the story that this world and its
few years are the only chance each of us has to do good, to
improve life just a bit for those around us, and to leave a
legacy of which we can be proud. Jews mostly tend to see
immortality in the ongoing life of family and community.

Our religious life is centered on two great cycles and
the intersections between them: the eternally repeat-
ing cycle of the week, the month, and the year, laden
with sacred days and *mitzvot,* and the inexorable march

of each individual human life from birth to death, also replete with occasions marked in sacred ways.

The Hebrew root that indicates holiness, *k-d-sh*, is one that links all of these; its presence woven throughout them tells us much about Jewish attitudes toward life and its ultimate values. Bear with me as we go through the multiple appearances of this verb stem as it becomes incarnate in four distinct but related nouns.

- *Kedushah* means "holiness." But it also refers to an event that forms the climax of every public Jewish worship service, both morning and afternoon (originally sunrise and sunset). It is the moment when we rise to join our voices to the angelic choir, overheard by Isaiah and Ezekiel as calling out each day: "Holy, holy, holy is Y-H-W-H of Hosts; the whole earth is filled with His glory!" and the mysterious "Blessed is the glory of Y-H-W-H from His place." Proclaiming God's holiness throughout the world is every Jew's daily task, to be accomplished in deed, in the way we live, but also by this proclamation in human language.

- *Kiddush*, "making holy," refers to the opening blessing of the Jewish Sabbath and holy days, recited over a brimming cup of wine. In the act of reciting these ancient words (even if we do so before sunset, when the Sabbath formally begins), we enter sacred time, accept the rest from work that protects that time, and promise to live with an extra measure of soulfulness for the coming day.

- *Kiddushin*, a plural form, refers to the marriage ceremony. "By this ring you are made holy to me," the bridegroom (and in many modern weddings, the bride as well) declares. Marriage is a promise to bring holiness into the intimacy of our lives as lovers, as committed partners, and as builders of a household. Jewish tradition views the marriage ceremony as its ideal celebration, the event that is copied or imitated in every other sort of celebration. This has much to do with the hope of bringing forth future generations, as indicated in the wedding blessings themselves. But Judaism fully embraces marriage for infertile as well as fertile couples and encourages adoption and nonparental involvement in the raising of children. "Whoever teaches another's child Torah, it is as though he [or she] had brought that child to birth." (This acceptance of nonreproductive marriage is the precedent for accepting same-sex marriage—a radically new idea, to be sure—in non-Orthodox Jewish circles in our day. The point of *kiddushin* is that the relationship be a holy one, defined by bringing God's presence into the home and manifest in the way the partners treat each other.)

- *Kaddish*, an Aramaic form of "holy," is an ancient prayer that for many centuries has been recited by mourners in the year after a death. It did not originate as a prayer for mourners, and it makes no mention of the dead, but rather it proclaims God's greatness and holiness in this world created by the divine will. It heaps words of praise upon the One Who is "beyond all blessings and songs, praises and beatitudes, recited in the world." *Kaddish* is recited only in the presence of a *minyan*, or quorum of ten Jews; the ability to stand up within the congregation to recite these words in the face of painful loss is respected by the community as a statement of faith, even an act of courage. To say it is to accept the reality of death and to declare one's commitment, in that moment, to the holiness of life and the obligation to bring forth holiness in this world. That commitment is to be strengthened rather than diminished by the loss one has suffered.

The linking together of these four words from the same root teaches us that Judaism's strength and inner wisdom have everything to do with the treasuring of life. We proclaim that life itself is a sacred gift and that God's presence is to be found in daily living. We exemplify that presence in human decency and kindness. God is glorified in the sacred moments that enrich the cycles of our years and lives, in the legacy that has carried us forward for so many centuries, allowing us to survive suffering and degradation with our heads held high. It is a legacy we are still here to teach, one that humanity still needs to hear us witness.

# 10

# EḤAD

## Hear O Israel

### There Is Only One

The best-known of all Jewish prayers, *Shema' Yisra'el*, is, in fact, not a prayer at all.

Prayers are typically addressed to God. Jewish prayers almost always contain the word *You*, spelled in English with a capital *Y*. "Blessed are You!" or "You are our Deliverer!" or "We call out to You!"

This line is addressed to the community: *"Hear O Israel"*—Listen, Jews!—*"Y-H-W-H is our God; Y-H-W-H is one!"*

How are we to understand Judaism's great proclamation of our monotheistic faith? Let us begin by asking a functional question, the most important question regarding human behavior. What *difference* does

monotheism make? One god, ten gods, a thousand—so
what? We Jews seem to put so much store in the fact that
we believe in one rather than many gods. Why? What is
the *payoff* of the great monotheistic revolution?

The only value of monotheism is to make you real-
ize that all beings, every creature—and that means the
rock and the blade of grass as well as your pet lizard
and your annoying neighbor next door—are all one in
origin. You come from the same place. You were created in the same great act of love, God bestowing God's
own grace on every creature that would ever come to
be. *Therefore*—and this is the key line, the only one that
really counts—*treat them that way!* They are all God's
creatures, just as you are. They exist only because of the
divine presence, the same divine presence that makes
you exist. Get to know them! Get to love them! Discover
the unique divine gift within each of them as well as the
common bond of existence that draws you all together.
Live in amazement at the divine light strewn throughout
the world. That's what it means to be a religious human
being. Even if you do not take the story of creation literally—and I, for one, do not—seeing this amazement and
wonder in all of existence is the beginning point of faith.

That is what the *Shema'* means by proclaiming
God one. But how do we render that mysterious name

Y-H-W-H, once badly reproduced in English as "Jeho-vah"? The mystical tradition within Judaism insists on translating God's name as "Being." Really it's not a name at all, not even fully a noun. Y-H-W-H is an impossible conflation of all the tenses of the verb "to be" in Hebrew. HYH means "was" in Hebrew; HWH indicates the present, "is;" YHYH would mean "will be." Put them all together and you get the implausible, and therefore mysterious, verb form Y-H-W-H. It prob-ably would best be translated as "Was–Is–Will Be." But since that's a little awkward to say each time, "Being" will have to do, a "Being" that embraces all of time and space as one, then reaches beyond them into impen-etrable mystery.

The meaning here is profound. "God" and existence are not separable from one another. God is not some entity over there who created a separate, distinct entity called "world" over here. There are not two; there is only one. The mystics insist on carrying monotheism that one step further.

To say you believe in one God but then to depict that God as an old fellow with a beard seated on a throne—or in any other single way, taken literally—is just a concentrated form of idolatry. It's like the old story where Abraham says to his father, "The big idol smashed all the others." You may remember learning the tale: Abraham's father Teraḥ had an idol shop. One day Papa was called away for a while and left his son in charge. Abraham smashed all the idols except the largest one, placing an axe in its hand. When Papa returned and saw the damage, Abraham explained, "The big idol destroyed all the rest!"

"Of course it didn't," Papa is supposed to have said. "It's only an idol."

"Aha!" cried out Abraham. And that "Aha!" was the beginning of the monotheistic revolution.[1] The same is true in each of our spiritual lives. If it's just about numbers, all you've got left is one big idol. Far too many people leave it at that. The real change has to be in the way you see existence itself.

In fact, the way you say "existence" in Hebrew is *HaWaYaH*, just a rearrangement of the four letters of God's secret name. To see God when you look at existence is a grand rearranging of the molecules. Seeing the *big* picture instead of the many smaller ones. God is Being when you see the whole picture, the way it all fits together, with the eyes of wonder. Of course we can't ever really see all of that big picture. The whole is infinitely more than the totality of its parts. Mystery remains.

But wait a minute. Then where did "the Lord" come from? Don't most translations read this verse as "Hear O Israel, *the Lord* our God, *the Lord* is one?" How did that get there?

Pronouncing the name Y-H-W-H aloud has been taboo since very ancient times. Supposedly only the high priest could say it, only on the holiest day of the year, and only in the holiest place, the Temple's innermost chamber. When the people in the courtyard heard it, they all fell on their faces. But the word Y-H-W-H appears multiple times on nearly every page of the Bible. How are you supposed to study and teach it if you can't say the word?

A little more than two thousand years ago, someone came up with a substitute. Every time the text says "Y-H-W-H," you say *Adonay*, which means "My Lord." It was an act of piety, a way of submitting, of saying "O Y-H-W-H, I am Your servant."

Now, to be a servant of Being is not a bad idea. It means to treat all existence with respect, to show a combination of love and reverence to each creature, to be a conveyor of universal compassion. Great! But something happened along the way. Once people started saying "Lord," they began to picture that elderly nobleman, the white-bearded white guy on a throne. They became *his* servants, not servants of Being, worshipping the image of God rather than the mystery behind it. How easily religion slides into idolatry!

This is the secret truth. Listen to one of the great sages, the Hasidic master Sefat Emet (1847–1905), who let this secret out of the bag in a letter he wrote to his children and grandchildren:

> The proclamation of oneness that we declare each day in saying Shema' Yisra'el needs to be understood in its true meaning. It is entirely clear to me … based on the writings of the great kabbalists … that the meaning of "Y-H-W-H is One" is not that He is the only God, negating other gods (though this too is true!), but that there is a deeper truth: there is no being other than God. This is true even though it seems otherwise to most people.… Everything that exists in the world, spiritual and physical, is God Himself. It was only because of the contraction [tzimtzum], willed by God that holiness descended rung after rung, until actual physical things were created out of it.
>
> These things are true without a doubt. Because of this, every person can be joined to God from any place, through the holiness that exists within every

single thing, even corporeal things. You only have to be negated (that is, to transcend the ego-self) in the spark of holiness.[2]

But now I have to turn back to the beginning of our non-prayer. "Hear O Israel." Who is "Israel" in this phrase?

Remember where the word comes from. Our ancestor Jacob once had an all-night wrestling match with an angel. A tough bird, that Jacob. Even an angel couldn't best him. When dawn came, the angel said, "Let me go! Time to sing God's praises!"

"Not a chance," Jacob said, "not until you bless me." So Jacob came out of that encounter with a new name: Israel, "Struggler with God."

That name has been carried by the Jewish people through history, and we bear it with pride. We don't have all the answers. Our notion of divine truth keeps growing and changing throughout our lives. But we struggle. It is the effort, the engagement, the not letting go of the question that makes us *Israel*, wrestlers with God.

But such a name cannot be the exclusive property of just a single human tribe. I believe that name belongs to all strugglers. Everyone who wrestles with angels, who struggles to make sense out of life, is part of some broader community called "Israel." There is an Israel defined by history, synonymous with the Jewish People. There is now a state of Israel as well, defined by its citizenry, including Jews, Arabs, and others. But there is yet another Israel, the undefined "nation" of all who seek and struggle.

*Shema' Yisra'el, Y-H-W-H Elohenu, Y-H-W-H eḥad!* "Listen, all you who struggle, all you who wrestle with life's meaning! Being is our God, Being is one!"

Don't look beyond the stars. There's no need to stretch your neck. God is right here, filling all of existence with endless bounty. Look around you. Look within. Open your eyes. Find God's presence in each and every creature and in the unified, transforming vision of all that is. *That's* what it means to belong to Israel, the people who struggle with God.

# Notes

## Chapter 1: Simḥah—Joy

1. *Likutey MoHaRaN* 2:23.
2. S. Y. Zevin, *Sippurey Hasidim* (Tel Aviv, 1959), p. 270.
3. b. *Sotah* 35a.
4. *Likutey MoHaRaN* 2:34, based on b. *Eruvin* 4a.

## Chapter 2: Tzelem Elohim—Creation in God's Image

1. y. *Nedarim* 9:5; 30b.
2. b. *Shabbat* 31a.
3. N. T. Mark 12:29–31.
4. m. *Yadayim* 3:5.
5. *Berakhot* 61b.
6. *Va-Yikra Rabbah* 34:3.
7. b. *Sanhedrin* 46b and Rashi to Deuteronomy 21:23.
8. *Bereshit Rabbah* 8:10.
9. Abraham Joshua Heschel, *The Circle of the Baal Shem Tov* (Chicago: University of Chicago Press, 1985), p. 118.

## Chapter 3: Halakhah—Walking the Path

1. b. *Shabbat* 133b.
2. b. *Sotah* 14a.
3. b. *Berakhot* 13a.
4. The derivation of *mitzvah* from the Aramaic *tzavta*, "together," is widespread in Hasidic sources. See, for example, *Degel Mahaneh Ephraim, korah*, in the name of the Ba'al Shem Tov.

## Chapter 4: *Tikkun 'Olam*—Repairing the World

1. Martin Buber, *Tales of the Hasidim* (New York: Schocken, 1947), p. 243.

## Chapter 5: *Shabbat*—Getting Off the Treadmill

1. b. *Hagigah* 15a.
2. y. *Rosh Hashanah* 3:5
3. m. *Hagigah* 1:8.

## Chapter 6: *Teshuvah*—Returning

1. Yom Kippur service, based on Ezekiel 18:23.
2. *Bereshit Rabbah* 22:13.
3. m. *Yoma* 8:9.

## Chapter 7: *Torah*—The People and the Book

1. b. *Baba Metzia* 59b.
2. m. *Makkot* 1:10.
3. *Zohar* 2:99a.
4. *Sefat Emet*, *Kedoshim* 1871, s.v. ba-Midrash.

## Chapter 9: *L'Ḥayyim*—To Life!

1. m. *Avot* 4:17.
2. m. *Avot* 1:3.
3. Moshe Haim Ephraim of Sudilkov, *Degel Mahaneh Ephraim*, Haftorah ki Tetze (Jerusalem: Machon Zohar V'Chassidus, 1995), p. 231.
4. Heard orally from Abraham Joshua Heschel.

## Chapter 10: *Eḥad*—Hear O Israel

1. *Bereshit Rabbah* 38:13.
2. Yehuda Leib Alter of Ger, *Otsar Mihtavim uMa'amarim* (Jerusalem: Machon Ga-haley Esh, 1986), pp. 75–76.

# Suggestions for Further Reading

I hope you have enjoyed this little volume, which is intended as a door opener to the great treasure house of Jewish teachings. Now that the door has been opened, where might you want to turn next?

If you like my particular approach to Judaism, you might want to look at some of my other books. *These Are the Words: A Vocabulary of Jewish Spiritual Life* is a Jewish spiritual vocabulary list made for beginners. It offers one-page explanations of 150 key Hebrew terms that you will want to understand. Use it either as a book to read through or as a handy reference tool. You will find more of my approach to questions of Jewish faith in *Seek My Face: A Jewish Mystical Theology*. If you want to know more about my reading of the mystical tradition, try *Ehyeh: A Kabbalah for Tomorrow*. All of these are published by and available through Jewish Lights. The fullest statement of my theology is found in *Radical*

*Judaism: Rethinking God and Tradition*, published by Yale University Press.

If you are a true beginner, or a non-Jew thinking about conversion, you might want to look at any of the following introductions to Judaism written from various perspectives along the Jewish spectrum: Lydia Kukoff, *Introduction to Judaism: A Sourcebook* (Reform), Michael Strassfeld, *A Book of Life: Embracing Judaism as a Spiritual Practice* (Havurah/Jewish Renewal, published by Jewish Lights), Simcha Kling and Carl Perkins, *Embracing Judaism* (Conservative), and *This Is My God* by Herman Wouk (Orthodox). Since much of the spirit of Judaism is intertwined with the Jewish calendar, consider checking out Irving Greenberg's *The Jewish Way: Living the Holidays* or Arthur Waskow's *Seasons of Our Joy* for explorations of Jewish ethical demands, practice, and spirituality through the lens of the holiday cycle.

Guides to Jewish practice are published by all the Jewish denominations and thus vary greatly. For a Reform approach, see Mark Washofsky's *Jewish Living: A Guide to Contemporary Reform Jewish Practice*. The Reconstructionist movement has a very thorough and systematic guide in the work of David Teutsch, *A Guide to Jewish Practice* (two volumes). For a Conservative point of view, check out Isaac Klein's *A Guide to Jewish Religious Practice* or Brad Artson's *It's a Mitzvah*. The movement has also recently published *The Observant Life*, a very thoughtful treatment of selected topics in Jewish observance. In the Orthodox community, there are many guides to Jewish observance. You might want to start with Hayim Donin's *To Be a Jew: A Guide to Jewish Observance in Contemporary Life* or Blu Greenberg's *How to Run a Traditional Jewish Household*, from the perspective of a Modern Orthodox Jewish woman. For a liberal guide to incorporating Jewish rituals and symbols into one's life, check out Anita Diamant and Howard Cooper's *Living a Jewish Life: Jewish Traditions, Customs and Values for Today's Families*. If you are interested in incorporating elements of personal spiritual practice into your daily life, look into Yitzhak Buxbaum's *Jewish Spiritual Practices*.

If you are looking for a variety of intellectual approaches to Jewish belief other than the ones expressed here (and any two Jews will indeed give you at least three opinions, as is well known!), you might try Michael Fishbane's *Judaism: Revelation and Traditions* or Arthur Hertzberg's *Judaism*. For sophisticated modern approaches that are still considered within the domain of Orthodoxy, have a look at David Hartman's *A Living Covenant: The Innovative Spirit in Traditional Judaism* (Jewish Lights) or Eliezer Berkovits's *God, Man, and History*.

Stories, including fiction, are a classic way to enter the mind-set of Jews and Judaism. Hasidic stories (I vouch for their wisdom, not for their historical accuracy) are a particularly useful tool for understanding Jewish values. I recommend the modern classic collection, Martin Buber's *Tales of the Hasidim*, as well as my friend and teacher Zalman Schachter-Shalomi's *A Hidden Light: Stories and Teachings of Early Habad and Bratzlav Hasidism* and *A Heart Afire: Stories and Teachings of the Early Hasidic Masters.*

For works of fiction, you might go back to the short stories of such masters as Sholom Aleichem, Isaac Bashevis Singer, and Shmuel Yosef Agnon. All were deeply rooted in the soil of Jewish tradition and knew how to mine it in creative and interesting ways. Let that be an inspiration to you!

Music is also an important way of entering the soul of Judaism. If you are a newcomer to Jewish spiritual music, try listening to Debbie Friedman's *Renewal of Spirit*, Shefa Gold's *Shir Delight: A Journey through the Song of Songs*, and David Zeller's *Aliveness*. For soulful music coming out of the mystical and Hasidic traditions you might want to explore the recordings of the Bratzlav Hasidim such as *Azamer Bish'vochin: Rebbe Nachman's Songs* or more contemporary music such as Shlomo Carlebach's

*The Gift of Shabbos* and *Songs of Peace*. Moving beyond words into the world of pure melody (*nigun*), listen to Michael Strassfeld's *Songs to Open the Heart*. Andy Statman's *Between Heaven and Earth* and *Songs of Our Fathers* and Joey Weisenberg's *Transformation of a Nigun* offer beautiful instrumental versions of *nigunim*. For a taste of different Jewish musical genres from around the world try *A Jewish Odyssey* on the Putumayo World Music label.

Many people around the world are turning toward meditation and mindfulness practices for spiritual enrichment. Here are some suggestions for resources from trusted Jewish leaders of meditation. Avram Davis collected an array of short essays on Jewish meditation from practitioners in his book *Meditation from the Heart of Judaism: Today's Teachers Share Their Practices, Techniques and Faith* (Jewish Lights). Sheila Peltz Weinberg's CD *Meditations for Jewish Spiritual Practice* leads the listener through guided meditations relating to the words of the prayerbook. If you are interested in connecting Jewish concepts to mindfulness practices, you may want to look into Jonathan Slater's *Mindful Jewish Living: Compassionate Practice*. A classic introduction to Jewish meditation is Aryeh Kaplan's *Jewish Meditation*. Other great resources include *The History and Varieties of Jewish Meditation* by Mark Verman and *The Handbook of Jewish Meditation*

*Practices: A Guide for Enriching the Sabbath and Other Days of Your Life* (Jewish Lights) by David Cooper.

There are also ever-growing collections of Jewish resources online. For articles and resources about a variety of topics related to Judaism and Jewish life, you may want to go to Myjewishlearning.com. If you are interested in short videos about the weekly Torah portion and other Jewish multimedia education resources for all ages, check out G-dcast.com. Ritualwell.com offers creative and contemporary Jewish rituals of all kinds. Two online resources for up-to-date news and culture about Israel and world Jewry are Tabletmag.com and TimesofIsrael.com. *Seventy Faces of Torah* engages a diverse selection of renowned rabbis and scholars to reflect on the weekly Torah portion in light of contemporary issues. The weekly column can be found at www.huffingtonpost.com/news/seventy-faces-of-torah.

**Arthur Green**, renowned spiritual leader, author and teacher, is one of the world's preeminent authorities on Jewish thought and spirituality. He is author of *These Are the Words: A Vocabulary of Jewish Spiritual Life*; *Ehyeh: A Kabbalah for Tomorrow* and *Seek My Face: A Jewish Mystical Theology*; among other books. He is the Irving Brudnick professor of philosophy and religion and rector of the Rabbinical School at Hebrew College in Boston.

> "Fresh and insightful.... An important read for all Jews, non-Orthodox and Orthodox alike.... This is a unifying book, that can bring all those who love Judaism, Torah, *mitzvot* and God together—all sharing in common the deepest ideas and desires for this world."
>
> —**Rabbi Asher Lopatin**, president,
> Yeshivat Chovevei Torah Rabbinical School

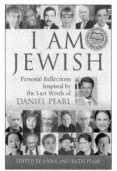

### Also Available

*I Am Jewish*
*Personal Reflections Inspired by the Last Words of Daniel Pearl*

**Edited by Judea and Ruth Pearl**

Being Jewish. What does it mean—today and for the future? Listen in as Jews of all backgrounds reflect, argue and imagine.

6 x 9, 304 pp, Deluxe Paperback w/flaps, 978-1-58023-259-3

*For People of All Faiths, All Backgrounds*
## JEWISH LIGHTS Publishing

www.jewishlights.com

 Find us on Facebook®
Facebook is a registered
trademark of Facebook, Inc.

Printed in the USA
CPSIA information can be obtained
at www.ICGtesting.com
JSHW021206280823
47391JS00004B/9